The author wrote the book as a form of healing and exploration of her own heart, her own emotions, and her own soul. Acknowledging her love for someone in the rawest sense of exposure and willingness to be vulnerable.. Working as a philanthropist, she has had the opportunity to meet many wonderful souls who have influenced her desire of exploration and healing and has helped guide her to understanding her own heart. She currently is a graduate student at Grand Canyon University in the addiction counseling program.

Âme Soeur

Amarra Handsome

Âme Soeur

Olympia Publishers
London

www.olympiapublishers.com

OLYMPIA PAPERBACK EDITION

A CIP catalogue record for this title is
available from the British Library.

ISBN: 978-1-80439-531-8

This is a work of fiction.
Names, characters, places and incidents originate from the writer's
imagination. Any resemblance to actual persons, living or dead, is
purely coincidental.

First Published in 2024

Olympia Publishers
Tallis House
2 Tallis Street
London
EC4Y 0AB

Printed in Great Britain

Dedication

dédié à mon amour

I

Toi

Deep in your gaze,
a body that nurtures,
housing my soul.

If I ask you,
would you fill in between,
where real meets blooming.

You are held close,
as a mountain held in fog,
subtle yet grounded.

Exist as you are,
as the space I rest in,
where I feel safe.

As your scent grows,
my reverence buds,
blooming in presence.

Your skin like cut grass,
let's me rest in the moment,
tumbling face forward.

Your eyes safe as home,
find me where I hesitate,
in the sight of truth.

Soaking your fingers,
you observed my form,
taming its oceans.

II

Moi

My energy moves,
as flow moves into stillness,
my awareness forms.

The secrets I keep,
protect the taste of your lips,
lips my dreams have known.

I let go,
feeling your existence,
sweetening my day.

The world erased me,
yet like a natural artist,
you painted me whole.

With little words,
so many simple truths live,
with much love for you.

My exposed heart,
like the sun is deeply warm,
and open to love.

III

Moi et Toi

The nature of us,
where origins are shadows,
have tuberous roots.

It's haunting,
falling blindly again,
in sweet surrender.

This distance,
inauspicious yet deep,
tiring yet safe.

A snapshot of time,
where chemistry is renewed,
wraps us freely.

Us from within,
drawn with the same ink,
disrobed and nourished.

The union of us,
unapologetically adhesive and raw.

Blooming from seed,
you are the kin of my soul,
implicate and warm.

People's biases,
a natural condition,
beyond all others.